ENERGY IN MOTION

ENERGY IN MOTION

STORIES AND LYRICS UNIQUELY MINE

JANEL

iUniverse, Inc.
Bloomington

ENERGY IN MOTION
STORIES AND LYRICS UNIQUELY MINE

iUniverse books may be ordered through booksellers or by contacting:

iUniverse
1663 Liberty Drive
Bloomington, IN 47403
www.iuniverse.com
1-800-Authors (1-800-288-4677)

ISBN: 978-1-4620-4060-5 (sc)
ISBN: 978-1-4620-4065-0 (ebk)

Printed in the United States of America

iUniverse rev. date: 07/27/2011

TABLE OF CONTENTS

ACKNOWLEDGMENTS

I would like to personally thank my husband and my daughter for reading and helping with the editing of my writing. I also want to thank my husband for the beautiful photographs I used for this publication. Both have been very supportive and helpful through this process. Love you guys.

I would like to thank my Mother for always encouraging me to write for my own enjoyment; also for being so supportive throughout my entire life. Thanks Mother for all you do.

I would like to thank my friends and family for allowing me to share so many of my written thoughts and ideas throughout the years.

I would be amiss if I did not mention a few of the many authors who have had a significant effect on my personal development throughout the years. I have read their books, listened to their tapes and CD's and attended their classes.

All these things I did while searching and seeking for the answers. Their words guided me to the realization that all the answers to my most important questions had to be answered by me. A heart felt thank-you to James Redfield, Ronna Herman, Eric Pearl, Neale Donald Walsch, Lee Carroll, Geoffrey and Linda Hoppe, Steve Rother, Hale Dwoskin, Esther and Jerry Hicks.

Love and Hugs
Jan

INTRODUCTION

You do not know me, but when you finish reading this book, you will know me better than most. When I chose to write about some of the most personal times of my life, I did so with the knowledge that there may be some questions about whether or not this is genuine. Well I hope to put all questions to rest before you begin reading the stories that affected me in such a personal way.

My experiences opened a new way for me to view my life, my beliefs and a new way for me to pursue my happiness. I believe that what I have found to be my truth is worth sharing. My hope is that you will find your truth and your happiness as well. I am not suggesting that I have found a better way simply another way.

It is another way to look at what has happened to you in your past and how it affects your present and may affect your future. What you do with the knowledge and wisdom you may gain is up to you. I'm not asking you to stop thinking or to stop questioning what you hear and read. And I'm not asking you to change. I am inviting you to expand your feelings about how you perceive yourself by asking who you are now and who do you want to be. If there is a change so be it but that will be entirely up to you.

Basically I would be honored to have you join me during a few moments of my sweet passage of time.

Jan Hein
(Janel)

ENERGY IN MOTION

Stories and Lyrics
Uniquely Mine

Have you heard the terms New Energy, New Consciousness, New Passion? Are you asking: What is this **new** concept?

Perhaps you ask "Why do I need to know anything *new* and why should I care"?

It has been my experience that the simple answer is, you don't need to *know* but you could choose to *care*! Then the choice to know even more becomes yours.

Now let's examine just for a moment what this means on a personal basis. Believe it or not you have the opportunity to choose whatever it is that interests you. When you begin to read a few paragraphs in a book, it might make your heart beat faster; it might feel like a *thread of truth* resonating through your body. That experience is the energy around you joining with you and that is experiencing **Energy in Motion.**

Therefore to expand on these ideas even further; imagine that you choose to live in the moment. As you bask in the sweetness you can also choose to allow the rest of the *energy in motion* to flow on by. Allowing the flow allows you to grow. Nothing gets stuck, so to speak.

In this concept, energy can be explained as feelings. They are feelings you can feel in your heart of hearts. Here are a few examples:

Energy in motion is when you have feelings inside that make you smile; for instance when you see a baby's first smile and that warm feeling creeps inside. Or when you see happy children playing, do you break out in a smile for no reason?

Here are a few of the things I have experienced that prove to me every day that energy is in motion. Feelings are experienced deep within where the energy begins to move.

I saw a double rainbow after the rain. The dark clouds brought every colored bow to life. I spotted white cranes flying in sync effortlessly under the fluffy white clouds. Robins flocked together to feed after an early spring ice storm. That is energy in motion.

Energy is moving every time you take a moment to notice what is happening around you. Just take the time to notice whether you are going to the grocery store or flying across the country.

That feeling you get inside can expand. It can expand because it is energy. You can expand it with a deep breath. Does that sound too simple? Don't knock it until you try it. You will feel it and once you choose to try expanding, there will be no way to stop it or explain it. Words of advice though, don't try to keep it. Take from it what you need to feel the joy then let it go, let it flow and let it expand way past who you think you are. When you do, you will know that you are a spiritual being having a human experience. You will know.

Do you like the sound of that? Then try it, in private or with someone you trust. The mystery disappears when you know it is just breathing. Take the time for yourself. If you don't, who else will? You deserve to feel happy, contented and loved.

Loving yourself in your heart of hearts will help you to understand how to love someone else. Remember that they also deserve to love themselves in their heart of hearts. When two people meet who have unconditional love for themselves, there is a special energy that flows between them and there is no other feeling that can compare. The flow continues; it does not stop; it does not leave behind emptiness because there is no end to the source.

If you feel emptiness, you know immediately that your energy has been taken but you received nothing in return. The flow stopped. Feel free to disengage from that person and you will immediately feel your own energy within your heart of hearts. You can continue your journey to find those who love themselves enough to share their energy with you. You will find it; wait for it; it is worth it.

Now the next time you see something that takes your breath away, take a moment to take a deep breath and feel the energy flow directly into your heart of hearts. There you can find unconditional love for yourself.

I wish you all the spectacular moments you need to find the love you deserve.

Now here is the other side of energy-*not*-in-motion. You have the choice of whether or not to find out more about what is happening around you energetically. If you choose to ignore the energy within and around you then you are resisting. Resistance can be painful and persistent. Energy that is not flowing throughout your body can become stuck and enhanced with pain the longer it remains in that state.

Personal experience has taught me resisting just does not work the way I thought it might and the whole process can be quite repetitive. I've heard this phrase repeated many times now: "What you resist persists." Have you heard it too?

When you see experiences in your life repeating over and over again, that is a very good signal to stop and choose again. One might say that your ultimate choice is to go with the flow or not! But remember you can always choose again.

Personally I choose to go with the flow. I call it my new normal. I hope you take the opportunity and choose to find out more about **Energy in Motion** for you.

The stories you are about to read reflect my journey into the discovery of all the energies surrounding me. Including those within me and how they interrelate with everyone I meet along the way.

I am excited to say that the journey you are about to embark on with me just might open you to new possibilities and new potentials as you reflect on my inner growth. I have a strong hunch it may be similar to yours. Similar in the sense that everyone has a story about their life, and most everyone talks about significant events in their life. That is why I decided to write part of my story here. You will see many *me, myself and I* references and maybe a few *you, yours, we and us* interlaced. That is my way of inviting you to take this journey with me.

I feel it is important to mention that I have had many questions, many doubts and many lesson to learn, just as you may have now. I have been taught that we are born with everything we know. Then we spend whatever time it takes to remember what we know and put it to good use.

My desire is that you will share in my experiences so that you will not only see the written words but hear the music within the lyrics and feel the energy that went into the creative writing. These stories reflect how my life started to change when I noticed that there was more to life than I originally thought. I might even say it drastically changed through experiencing some good, some bad and some ugly *energy in motion*. But I'm getting ahead of myself; allow me to start at the beginning of my awareness of the amazing energies around me.

It all started when my husband's son gave me a book of fiction called The Celestine Insights by James Redfield. For more information about his work please feel free to visit his website. www.celestinevision.com

The book seemed a bit strange to me at the time but I decided to read it with an open mind and see what happened. What I didn't count on was that it reached inside of me and started prodding me when I wasn't paying attention. Later, I found out that this is called *waking up*. Since I had already made the choice to have an open mind it worked on me day and night until I had to read all his books as well as the companion workbook.

As I diligently read through the material I started to realize some things about myself. I realized that I was starting to change. Right you may have guessed it, I'm not a fan of change but I began to notice the little things first. I began to understand my greatest fear was being *alone* and I discovered that once I was aware of it and brought it out into the open I began to accept it. With this acceptance I started to feel better physically. Oh I still had aches and pains but other things like colds and flu were not as bad as they used to be. I liked that. I thought "This is good!"

Along with my health my attitude was changing. I didn't feel it was necessary to be sarcastic in attempts to be funny. I even started noticing when my *hot buttons* were being pushed. *Injustice* was a big one for me. Any kind of injustice would make my blood boil and that affected how I felt physically as well. Once I had the awareness, I could stop overreacting to some of the issues that came up in my daily living. It did take time for me to find ways to express how I was feeling about these changes and I did a great deal of research about the new energy concept and that brought me back to a more personal and inner search. I had to find what would work for me. I had to find ways to let go of the emotions. I had to find a way to allow my bad experiences to become memories without the emotion.

Finally the memories no longer have a physical effect on me. I have let them go and moved on. I believed and still believe that letting go is one of the main reasons my health improved. I was no longer holding on to everything that bothered me. I began to notice that the time between feeling an emotion and allowing it to leave me physically became shorter and shorter.

About this same time as my heart began to open, my mind began to clear and I was inspired to write. Together my heart and mind worked perfectly in sync with the energies around me and within me. When my heart and mind worked separately, I would have blockages and I would not be able to think of the words that clearly reflected how I was feeling.

I always remind myself even to this day, about the Mind and Heart Connection when I begin to feel an inspiration to write. I might add that I find it is a good idea to remind myself about the connection whenever I open my mouth to speak as well. Words can be so powerful that all good deeds go by the wayside if an ill thought comment is overheard by someone nearby. One of my main goals for writing is to show how words can embrace and help others to feel better about their lives.

If you are thinking that my lyrical writing will be long and complex, you can forget that notion right now. All my writing is inspired by what I have been taught and the main theme has always been Keep It Simple Student (KISS). As you continue reading you may also discover a childlike cadence to my writing and my lyrics. That is exactly how my inspiration comes to me. It is as though I am hearing it through the mind and heart of a child. For me the inner child plays an important role in my method of expressing.

As I began to write, my poems and lyrics came from wanting to know what else was available for me. I mentioned before that my experiences could be described as good, bad and ugly. For me, the *good* was finding answers when I didn't know the question. The *bad* reflected my uncertainty; my concern, anxiety and stress; the *ugly* expressed my hardships such as loss and grief. These themes appear throughout all my poems and lyrics.

I began to explore what was available for me by reviewing what I had been reading. I went back to the discovery that one of my greatest fears was being alone. I decided to do what it would take to help myself feel more secure in my own world and in my everyday living. As I was finding new versions of aspects of myself every day, I found that the mother in me and the wife in me both needed my attention. Both aspects had memories of being alone.

It was profound when I discovered that all I needed was a change in my perception of the word *alone*. That was when I separated the syllables in the word al-one and it became *all-one*. I found that a simple change in my perspective changed the way I felt about myself, even when I was alone or feeling lonely.

The poem *Alone-All One* reflects those feelings I had about being alone and then the discovery that even being alone can lead to peace.

ALONE—ALL ONE

Sometimes when I feel alone,
My heart feels empty.
There is fear and pain
With no thought of gain

I take a moment to go inside,
And listen to the rhythm of my heart,
I find the answer.
I discover I am not alone,
I am All-One.

My heart is filled with Love
So very deep inside
I wonder as Love expands,
It overflows to me and you.

When I am ready,
I will change my view
This simple truth can heal.
And it does so very well.

Writing had become my release, my way of letting go of issues that were no longer important in my life. I had discovered that in order for me to heal in every way I had to choose to take the steps I thought were necessary to accomplish my goal. I discovered that I could write about my feelings in order to keep the energy flowing. The energy within and around me was no longer becoming stuck or stagnate. It felt amazing as though my truth was being expressed through every word I wrote.

Of course this new knowledge had to stand the test of time. In 1996 I lost my older sister to a sudden brain bleed. The whole family was devastated. I felt like I had been hit in the chest. After that let up a bit, I felt like I was hit in the stomach. That feeling went on for a very long time. I prayed every day that I would stop hurting so much. I prayed that the tears would go away and only the good memories would remain. Writing did not even enter my mind during these hurtful, ugly times of suffering. I felt alone in a room full of people.

One dark night as I lay in my bed with my eyes closed trying to hold back the tears I felt a very soft *touch* like a kiss on my cheek and heard a voice in my head that said "I'm all right, you don't have to worry. I can be with you any time you want me near." I quickly opened my eyes and looked around in the dark but of course there was nothing to see. It was all in that *feeling place* I had found where I felt safe.

That experience helped me in so many ways. Immediately I felt a lifting off my chest as though a load of weight was removed from my heart. Once I was better able to cope with losing a loved one so early in life, my awareness helped me cope with other aspects of my life as well. Most of all I felt comfort in the knowledge that she was so near. That experience changed how I perceived death and dying. I was eager to find out more.

Several years later while I attended a writing class at my local University, I found I was ready to write and express how I was affected by my sisters passing. I decided to write down my thoughts to help me and perhaps help other members of my family as well. The poem *When You Left* tells the story of how I was feeling during and leading up to the 'touch.'

WHEN YOU LEFT

The clocks are still going but will never be the same
When you passed we were just
getting to know each other
Days of sister battles had ended and
the laughter had begun
We had a distance between us
that was getting smaller
as your big sister role changed to friend

We all said good bye at the funeral that day
I saw the families of the children you taught,
who came to share our grief
I felt the sorrow of family and friends
I tolerated sad wishes at the celebration of your life
How wonderful you were,
how much you would be missed
My heart was breaking; felt like it would never mend
I knew from when Daddy passed
that this could last awhile
We went our separate ways in search of what could heal
There was nothing we could say to help one another

Each night, when missing you became too strong,
I would shed a tear
The memories were clear,
as was the fact you were not here
I prayed for a sign to help ease the pain,
and little by little it came
A touch, like a kiss on the cheek, and
I heard "Don't worry, I am fine"

The next year, 1997 proved to hold another test as well. One day in the very early morning hours, our two beloved pet dogs scampered through an open gate and got lost in a rain storm. After three days and a lot of help from officials, I finally found the male Toby. He had been with us nearly six years and was the mate of the female Sheeba. After months of endless searching, we were unable to find her. Sheeba had been given to us as a gift from my husband's daughters and she had been with us for eight years and had given birth to three litters of pups. I was looking forward to all of us enjoying our golden years together.

Searching for Sheeba became an obsession for me. Finally after talking with pet psychics, *yes I was that desperate,* who assured me that she had not crossed over, I decided to think of her as being in a good home with people who loved her and took very good care of her. The memories of the long searches and what I could have done differently kept popping up in my mind. I would feel a *tearin*g in my chest and the tears would form. It was like losing a family member or a best friend and I had an extremely difficult time dealing with not knowing where she was. I was hoping for reassurance that she was happy wherever she might be.

For days and days thoughts of her kept coming to mind whenever I was driving my car home from work. I even thought I saw her one day while riding the city bus, but I could not be sure it was her and I had a large load of papers I was taking home. I still wondered if I had missed my opportunity to find her. I kept reminding myself of how well cared for that dog had appeared even though it was heart wrenching to think it might have been her.

Several years later on a sunny day as I was driving home, I came over the usual hill and had this overwhelming sensation to say 'good bye' to Sheeba. It was so strong and so unusual that I knew in that moment something drastic had happen; she had crossed over. It was a feeling that I just *knew* but could not explain. That moment of joining with her spirit helped me understand that she was okay. I could visualize her scampering and jumping, playing in the wind. A peaceful solace came over me. She was finally home again.

The lyric *Come Back Little Sheeba* reflects some of these moments and memories.

COME BACK LITTLE SHEEBA

The clock struck 6:30 that day
It was dark and gloomy
A thunder shower was on its way
I stretched and thought
What a great day to sleep-in

A feeling of concern urged me up
Were the dogs safe in the garage?
The fan had fallen over in the doorway
The yard gate stood open wide
Not a good sign.

What happened on that dreary day they
Scampered through the opened gate?
An adventure in the neighborhood?
Frightening thunder until they ran too far?
I called for Toby; I called for Sheeba,
Until I could no more

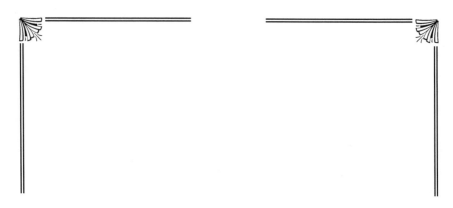

A miracle came days later, I received a call,
Only one was spotted, not too far away
Relieved, I found Toby hungry and tired
I tried not to show concern for his mate

I remembered . . . .
Laughing while she danced and we played
A game around the yard, calling
Come back little Sheeba,
Come back little Sheeba

At night I would cry and Toby would howl
For months we searched
And searched all around

Never to be found

In 1998, a year after the missing pet episode I ended up in the hospital for ten days with some unknown viral infection running through my body. The only thing the doctor said was that something was attacking every organ except for my brain and heart. It was a long process and I ended up losing a lot of weight very fast, the hard way.

Prior to my hospitalization I had a very strange experience. I could only describe it as an experience with an Angel, well angel *wings* anyway. As I was lying in bed for the night I began to get the chills. They became more and more severe until I could no longer hold still. I was very groggy and pretty much out of it with the shaking and the only thing I could think of was I wanted to get warm. After a while I was trying desperately to get warm. All of a sudden I *felt* a slapping sensation around the front of my body. It felt like there was something coming from behind me that wrapped around in front of me and whacked me on my upper arms and chest. The slapping persisted until I finally came around enough to know that I needed to ask for help.

The time spent in the hospital was very lonely because I was isolated from other patients due to the nature of my illness. Since they did not tell me specifically what it was, I had to assume it could have been contagious.

In time after I recovered from my illness, it occurred to me that I could have died. That moment allowed me to understand that at some level I knew I had made the conscious choice to live. I knew this was a profound and very important choice. I felt so strongly that I was being reminded of my God given gift of free will. I had a choice to make and I made it.

With this awareness about my choices, I felt the urge to find what else there might be available for me to discover. I do not remember consciously asking the questions about who am I or why I am here. I do remember years before when I was making a conscious choice about my future, asking the question "Isn't there anything better than this?" But then I felt very sure that question had already been answered when I chose to leave an abusive relationship. I had gotten out of a toxic relationship and into a new loving relationship and was feeling quite content.

So when I found out about *choices* and how they would affect my life in a very significant way, I tried to apply that knowledge to past situations and current ones. It took me a few more years to find out how significant that discovery would be for me.

Now back to the time when I was so rudely awakened by something very weird. Strangely enough the whacking sensation I had experienced kept reappearing in my visualization as being wings. I had no idea why I kept revisiting those thoughts. I did not feel comfortable asking anyone what it could have been. I didn't want to end up on someone's couch, if you know what I mean. I decided to confide in my friends I had come to trust. I also listened to my own inner voice, deep within my heart.

Eventually, I discovered that the answer or the explanation was completely up to me. Apparently my belief system was coming through very strong and my belief was that the wings slapping around me was my Self, my inner angel, my Higher Self alerting me to the problem. How does anyone know for sure about strange occurrences like that, other than what they can believe just might be the answer. Whatever the case, I am still very grateful for that powerful intervention.

After recovering a bit from the hospital stay and trying to gain some strength back after losing 40 pounds, I began to think of this experience as a choice I had made and that led me to the conclusion that I was to enjoy every day as though it was precious. The following lyrics kept repeating themselves to me, I had made a choice and I heard the words *I want to live*.

I WANT TO LIVE

I want to Live, yes live
In the Morning
In the Evening
In the NOW

When the days look so bleak
When the pain is so strong
Then I choose, yes I choose
I choose Life, yes Life

Let the Sun shine in
Let the Wind blow through
There will be love all around
And I'll know, yes I'll know
When it's for me

I want to Live, yes live
In the Morning
In the Evening
In the NOW

Every day did become precious to me and as the years went by I had many experiences that continued to change my way of thinking. My discoveries were deeply personal and I received huge insights. I had discovered how to follow my ***thread of truth*** through reading books by a variety of amazing authors. I described my thread of truth as the way I used discernment while reading and learning new concepts. Discernment became very important to me because there was a lot of material available that did not follow my thread of truth. I had listened to numerous tapes and CD's, gone to workshops, seminars and training sessions and I found and continue to find that my thread of truth leads me to very interesting times in my life.

I have always been drawn to the new ideas being presented since 1999. My discernment led me to authors who encouraged me to think for myself and to apply what resonated within me and simply disregard the rest of the information. That process allowed me to be less confused about all the information and more comfortable in the knowledge that I could choose for myself. That is when I became aware that I am drawn to the new energy way of living. That includes discovering new possibilities and new potentials. I am also drawn to the belief that my desire to experience life, expand knowledge and express experiences fulfills my Soul's desire as well.

I have become very interested in sharing my lyrical messages as an avenue of expression and peacefulness for myself and for others as well. I feel many changes within me and as mentioned before, I can *hear* words of comfort and inspiration that I have been compelled to write down. I believe that many of the messages have reflected a change in my evolutionary growth. Some of the messages are accompanied with a simple melody; some are words for others who are in need and some are simply fun. I feel as though my mind and heart are full of sounds needing to be expressed.

This book has become one of the avenues for me to express my experiences and share my lyrics with others. When energy is in motion, there is no limit to where it can go and no limit on where it can come from. I began to notice I was more open to what was happening all around the world. It became important to me to send loving energy to anywhere it might be needed. I did not to put limits on the energy because to me energy was limitless. I simply incorporated the practice of expanding the loving energy I felt and allowed it to flow.

One day a dear friend of mine called and related to me that she was in a deep state of hurt and confusion after being betrayed by someone she loved. I had this overwhelming desire to help her but so very little can be said at times like these, other than being a supportive friend. Later a poem came to me that expressed how every day we have to make choices about how we are going to treat others and how we are going to accept how we are treated. I wanted her to be able to hold on to something tangible during her time of need. So I printed up the poem I'd written based on the letters C.A.L.L. I continue to dedicate this poem to my friend. It is *Answer the CALL*

ANSWER THE CALL

Every day we awaken to new possibilities
Every day we choose what to experience

When we follow our Soul's desire, we choose
C-ompassion, **A**-llowing, **L**-ife and **L**-ove
When we follow our Soul's desire;
we answer the C-A-L-L

Compassion is the choice
to honor all that we experience,
Darkness and the light
Allowing is the choice
to honor all there is on The Earth,
Universe and the Omniverses
Life is the choice
to experience everything in its fullness,
Bad and the good
Love is the choice
to Love ourselves completely,
Unconditionally,
Only then can we love others as ourselves

When we listen to the CALL,
we feel protected, secure,
We have no fear
When we answer the CALL,
we find true happiness within

~

I can remember very distinctly the first time I heard a lyric and music in my head blended together. I had been practicing releasing health related issues. During that time, I became aware of a particular need that I had and it was to simply stop for a moment; take a deep breath, relax and discover what energies might be floating nearby. Everything I was experiencing was so new to me that I was not clear on what the questions were let alone understand how I would recognize the answers. Even though I did not understand everything about the concept at the time, the words and the melodies that evolved from those first moments of going within were very sweet. They appeared to me through the poem called *Take a Moment.* This poem speaks of my discovery of an inner self awareness.

TAKE A MOMENT

Take a Moment,
Go Inside
Take a Moment,
Listen to your Heart

Take a Moment, Go Inside
The Answer is in your Heart, My Friend
The Answer is in your Heart

Take a Moment,
Go Inside
Take a Moment,
Listen to your Soul

Take a Moment, Go Inside
The Answer is in your Soul, My Friend
The Answer is in your Soul

Take a Moment,
Go Inside
Take a Moment,
Listen to your Self

Take a Moment, Go Inside
The Answer is Within You, My Friend
The Answer is Within

~

The next lyric called *The Calming* became a meditation for me to calm all the energies around me. In essence it prepared me for taking a moment and going inside and finding peacefulness through the simple process of breathing. Deep breathing is a common thread throughout my writings. This simple little lyric physically takes me to a place of relaxation and is very effective as a recording. Breathing deeply and releasing slowly calms my mind and body in order to be at a comfortable state of rest. I have used this method many times when my mind would not stop racing through the events of the day. I hope you find that this poem will give you a moment of rest as well.

If you have serious health issues or have trouble breathing, check with your doctor before beginning any new program.

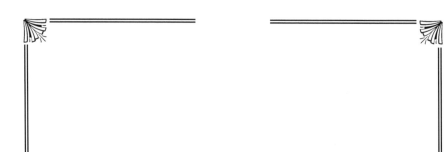

THE CALMING

Breathe deeply, release slowly
Breathe deeply, release slowly
Breathe deeply, release slowly

Take a moment, Go Inside
Take a moment, Listen to your breath
Take a moment, Go Inside
The Calming is in your breathing my dear
The calming is in your breath

Breathe deeply, release slowly
Breathe deeply, release slowly
Breathe deeply, release slowly

Mother Nature has a way of sending amazing 4D pictures of *energy in motion* like no other source could possibly match. Through the seasons I've seen the amazing winter wonder landscapes with impossible sculptures of waves and drifts of snow. And the sparkling beauty of an icicle formed by the slow dripping off a roof top. The picture of spring flowers blooming in random, building a blanket of colorful beauty that cannot be out shined by a rainbow. The summer fields of green and gold and flaxen blue that spread for acres on end. The layer of fall colors on the changing leaves before they depart from their perches high above the ground. There is great beauty all around and I have learned to enjoy the moments every time I see them.

There was a day when something so spectacular and yet so simple happened that it inspired an overflowing of emotion from the depths of my Soul.

It was a particularly windy fall day as I was driving through town; I noticed the leaves flying around high up on the wind. They began swirling in circles. Then the swirls appeared different, not the usual circles on the ground. The leaves would start swirling at ground level and then began lifting up and up, higher and higher to the top of the trees right in front of me. It took my breath away I had never seen leaves swirl in circles straight up into the air like that. I have never seen them do it quite like that again. The scene filled my heart with overflowing warmth and a lyrical poem was the result. The music I heard was a rendition of John Denver's <u>Annie's Song</u>. As the scene and melody unfolded so did the words to *Dance with the Energy*.

DANCE WITH THE ENERGY

Dance with the Energy
Like leaves in the Wind
It is so peaceful
To Feel it within

Dance with the Energy
Like snowflakes in Motion
It is so wonderful
To Feel the Emotion

Dance with the Energy
That swirls like the Wind
It is so peaceful
To Feel You Within

Yes I have discovered that energy plays a very important part of my life. I hope you are discovering it as well. I know that everything is energy; therefore being aware of how it feels enables me to have a better understanding of myself as well as others. I am an energy being, you are an energy being, all of nature is energy. Energy is in the rocks, pebbles, stones and boulders; dirt and grass, trees and all their inhabitants as well. I know that everything I can imagine is energy.

Science teaches us that energy is a part of everything and everything has its own ecosystem. If there is an imbalance in nature it does everything in its power to find resolution. Nature's urgency *is* balance. Nature balances energy by changing the landscape with wind, water, fire and earthquakes. Our bodies also feel the urgency to have balance.

For instance when I feel an imbalance on the inside, I can end up with a cold or stomach flu. I believe that this discomfort is the result of the energy becoming stuck within me. Remember the words *let it flow?* I was and am very well aware that it is difficult to remember those words while in the midst of a bad cold or flu episode, but I just try to remember to choose to feel better soon. Then I go about the business of treating the symptoms. I believe that when I choose to feel better soon, I allow the energy to flow and the mind, body and heart connect to offer me the balance I need to heal. My experience has been that the balance will emerge and the discomfort will fade away as quickly as it came.

Following are some lyrics I wrote that may help you find the balance you desire. I hope that these words will not only be heard but that you will feel the energy as well, then finding the resolution within you becomes a labor of love. *Energy Expressed* is a lyric that explained to me how everything is energy and how it continues to expand and flow.

ENERGY EXPRESSED

Welcome the Energy
Be open to it
It already knows where to go
Let it flow, Let it be
Play with the Energy
That swirls in the breeze
Play with the energy
And Feel it with ease
It already knows where to go
Allow it to go on its way
Welcome it
Open wide to it
Let it be fully Expressed

To continue with the thought about energy expanding and flowing, it is important to remember that energy also seeks balance in our bodies through our energy centers. *Rainbow in Your Soul* explains my perception of how the energy flows through our physical form and activates within us at the various energy centers. Those of you who are familiar with chakras and meridians will understand the significance of being aware of your energy within and allowing it to continue to flow unrestricted. Each energy center is associated with a color. I believe that these beautiful colors that reside within us can be perceived as a rainbow shining light within for ourselves and in some cases for all to see.

This is an exercise in balance and is very effective when recorded in your own voice.

RAINBOW IN YOUR SOUL

The colors of the rainbow
Are swirling around us
Red, orange, yellow, green,
Blue, indigo and violet white

Each is an entity unto itself
Together they create the whole.
Listen my dear and you will see
What this rainbow of color can truly be.

Feel the golden glow arising within
It is the light that truly binds
Let it keep you steadfast with the earth

Do you feel the brilliant red
As it swirls with the gold
Let it keep you safe and bold

Do you feel the electric orange
As it swirls with the red
Let it help you be alive and create

Do you feel the sun-filled yellow
As it swirls with the orange
Let it help you be who you are

Do you feel the pulsing green
As it swirls with the yellow
Let it always open within your heart

Do you feel the radiating blue
As it swirls with the green
Let it help you speak your dream

Do you feel the majestic indigo
As it swirls with the blue
Let it give you knowledge as a jewel

Do you feel the white violet halo
As it blends with the gold
Let it join your Human and your Divine

Do you feel the rainbow around you
As it swirls back to the earth
Let it keep you safe as a new babe at birth

At this point in my story I was well into my journey to locate what I thought I longed for the most. I called it **enlightened contentment**. My searching at this point was to find out who I'd become so that I could understand where I'd been. I understood the concept of the relationship between experiences, beliefs and aspects and concluded that I should continue to search inside for all the pieces of myself. I found the adult in me and chose to keep a level head. That concept was important to me because I had been told many times: "Get your head out of the clouds." I wanted to be sure that I was grounded for all my new experiences.

During my inner search I remembered the child I had been. I discovered that the feeling of those innocent years felt very refreshing. I did not want to lose that innocence when I was finding my connection to my spirit. I wanted to view each new experience as though I was seeing it through the eyes of a child.

Life had taught me to expect the worst and I wanted to be able to expect the best in humanity. Even when horrific tragedy happened in the world, I wanted to be able to see the miracles that came in the aftermath. I wanted to be focused on helping others see the miracles as well. I wanted to be able to understand what was happening to all those precious souls that gave their life so that others could continue to live. I was convinced that the time had come to focus on the love in our hearts and allow the fear and hate to dissolve.

When I found my inner child I learned to play again. I knew how very important it was to find my inner child's imagination and let it soar. Try it I know you will like it.

The lyric *The Inner Child* reflects my process of finding a way to view all that was new in my life as though I was seeing it through the eyes of a child.

THE INNER CHILD

Oh the longing for the inner child
That used to play in my heart
Day after day after day

Where is the fun, the joy, the laughter?

The child feels contained by the adult in me
Like a seedling that is so tender
That needed a soft place to rest
Now it is time to grow

The spirit in me understands the miracles
The child sees no limits in love
Anything can happen, and it does

Where is this inner child?
Why does it hide?
Where does it go?

In my golden moments
When the wisdom flows
I feel the child dwelling between
The Adult and the Spirit of me

I spent a great deal of time remembering the experiences, identifying the beliefs and honoring the aspects of me that had helped form who I had become. My beliefs were deeply etched within me from my childhood experiences through my adult experiences. My beliefs determined how I thought and how I reacted to other people.

Through a great deal of searching and finding the process that resonated with what I held true, I was able to let go of my old baggage cloaked in beliefs. Letting go allowed me to have new ideas, new beliefs and new discoveries. These new discoveries led me in new directions. I began to notice that I felt so much lighter and freer to explore different avenues that I had never thought of before. I was ready to leave my cozy little comfort zone. I found I could explore all these new ideas without compromising my traditions or my ethics. In many cases the new directions led me to have new perceptions about my traditions and I found greater and deeper meaning to the word family. I was convinced that my views were enhanced because of my new perceptions on life. The word *responsibility* became even more important at this time in my life.

Call it an *aha m*oment or a great revelation because all of a sudden I realized I was responsible for my own world. I was the one who brought everything into my life.

I also knew I am the one who can change and I am the one who can choose. I am the one who can have a deep heartfelt love for my Self and share it with everyone in my life. I knew I could strive to combine all my aspects and personalities whether they were good or bad.

I understood that all I had experienced in the past and all my present and future experiences would make me whole. It was so clear to me and I knew I had to know these things in order to be complete.

I was able to accept that I could love myself in spite of what I may have done in the past or what may have happened to me. I discovered that everything I have ever done was really a *great experience*. I should not punish myself for experiencing life the way it was presented to me. Those experiences were my great lessons in life. Those experiences were not supposed to stop me, they were supposed to encourage me to keep going and not look back. I needed to stop telling myself I was not worthy of looking forward.

I was finally able to let my imagination soar and it felt good. It felt like it was going inter dimensional. That led me to believe that I was able to create my own heaven on earth. The lyrics in *Imagination* helped me see the potentials available to me and all I had to do was connect the dots between my mind, body and soul. This connection has been referred to as my Body of Consciousness and those words resonated very deeply with me.

IMAGINE

Just Imagine what you could do
Let the dreams come alive
It will all be for you
You will know how to live
Yes you'll know life

Are your dreams filled with strife?
Do you let them flow?
Do they cut you like a knife?
Let it go, let it go

There's potential all around
Let it flow, Let it flow
You will find the highest truth
And you'll know, yes you'll know

Just Imagine what you could do
Let the dreams come alive
It will all be for you

You will understand life,
Yes you'll know how to live
Life is all about you.

Once my heart was filled with love and compassion for myself it made perfect sense that all the love and compassion in me was over flowing. I knew my compassion could touch everyone I was close to. I felt that even those who would pass by me while shopping or walking their dog would sense the energy coming from my smile. In fact many people would smile back at me as though they knew the secret; the secret that love and compassion comes from inside our heart of hearts. I felt so close to everybody and I had a deep heartfelt hope that everybody could feel what I was feeling.

Even when I would write I felt that the words came directly from my soul, my spirit and I understood that I could not pass judgment on anyone for anything. I understood that I could not pass judgment on any aspect of myself either. I could only feel compassion for all my feelings even the feelings of guilt and self loathing.

It was surprising to me that at that moment of clarity I felt enlightened; then I felt contentment. *Connect With Yourself* revealed a fun way of my having a conversation with myself saying it was okay to feel a variety of emotions. This helped me understand that feelings were a gift to treasure and I should finally welcome all feelings into my life.

CONNECT WITH YOURSELF

Today seems full of gloom
The Energy is trying to get through
Feel It knocking at your Energy door
Ah, yes there it is.

Now sense the Energy flowing through
Does it seem to stop anywhere?
Let it Flow Within
Ah, yes there it is.

Feel it connecting your toes to your nose
Feel it connecting your feet to your seat
Feel it connecting your knees to your ears
Ah, yes there it is.

Today now seems full of Joy
The energy got through!
I felt it knocking at my door
Ah, yes there it is.

Enlightened contentment is contagious. My awareness of those around me brought exciting results. People were smiling at me as though they knew me. Tiny babies would look at me and giggle with delight. I'd never had that effect on babies before, other than my own of course. Then I realized that they appeared different to me because I had opened my heart and had deep compassion for them. People can actually feel that in another person. I felt so fortunate to be able to know what that was like. But I knew and understood that I cannot change the journey for anyone else.

It was so difficult for me to keep my enthusiasm in check but I knew many were not ready to hear what I had to say. It might even cause people to be afraid of my words, even though my discovery was for myself. They had to find out for themselves just as I did. In fact I can remember when I was a teen telling my parents that I had to find out about life for myself. I don't remember what the situation was, but I remember those words.

And still I found myself time and time again wishing there were ways to get through to others about how I felt about life and living. I wanted everybody to know how my changes had affected me in such significant ways.

I was grateful for my writing because it had become one avenue to reach others, but it could not reach everyone. That was the main reason I continued to expand the energies I felt and I trusted they would reach where they were needed the most.

That was my passion; to allow love and compassion to flow through me and out to all who were in need whether they were in my close circle of family and friends or on the other side of the world.

I believe that there are no boundaries for energy and everything is *Energy in Motion*. My passion has become an act of kindness in the form of empowerment to others so that they can find their passion too.

The poem *Passion* is a simple little no nonsense lyric about my feelings.

PASSION

I feel the safe space around me
I feel the safe space within me

I can create with intent and emotion,
This is my Universal Expression.

This is my Vision
This is my Heart song
This is my Joy

This is my Emotion
Hear me Roar

This is my PASSION
It is ME Breathing Yes
I AM here to share

It was very clear to me that everyone must find their own inner strength; their own passion in life; even their own connection to divinity. I looked forward to the day when everyone would feel that everything is perfect just as it is while they continued on their journey.

You may be asking, "What do I do with *enlightened contentment* once I find it?"

That will be up to you. That is how it should be. Stay within that moment until you feel you want to move on. It feels very safe, blissful and peaceful to dwell within the real you.

There are many ways to find what is meaningful on a personal level. I started with one of my *hot buttons* and then expanded on that thought until I found my way of expressing myself.

You are reading about it here in this little book. Many of my lyrics and messages express how I continued to experience my *enlightened contentment.*

The journey only required that I love and trust my Self and feel **within** like I had never felt before. I had to feel deeper than my physical heart. So I thought of it as the sacred heart chamber deep within my soul. I felt it within my very core, even in my cells. As I was hearing the words I felt as though they were coming from my Soul connection with a higher Source.

At first I thought of the connection as being with God. My perception of God was of a father figure and sometimes as a friend. That was very comforting for me because I did not have to take responsibility for what I was writing. But that would mean I did not have to be conscious about what I was writing. That did not seem like a good partnership if I did not know what I was doing. What if I wrote something that was hateful or hurtful, would I not know that and if I did write it anyway would I be punished by an angry God?

I did pray that I would gain some clarity or insight about this dilemma going on in my head and that is when it became clear that I was an extension of God in a much bigger and infinite way. I remembered that I had a God seed within me that could be ignited. I had to wrestle with this concept for a while because of my belief systems but I was also willing to have an open mind about all my perceptions of creation and creating.

After it became clear to me that I was responsible for what I was writing, it took me some time to digest what that meant. How could I feel that I was responsible when I depended upon God to guide me? If not God then who could it be?

That was when I remembered the simple concept that God created me in his likeness. I put that together with knowing that our free choice required responsibility and both were gifts from God. There are no boundaries for God just like there are no boundaries for energy. I remembered that God could experience life through me. That likeness meant to me that God was within me and not somewhere outside telling me what to do.

I had to combine all three thoughts: my willingness to believe that I had free choice and that I was responsible for everything I brought to myself, with the knowledge that the God within me was my guiding light.

Without that sacred light of God within me I would be without the love and compassion I knew to be true. This is when the lyrics became very intense for me and that in itself expresses how I was feeling when writing this message from God called *Divine Energy Expressed*.

DIVINE ENERGY
EXPRESSED

Do you know how wonderful you are
Do you see your shining beauty

Do you feel how safe you are
Not for your ego to enjoy alone

Feel it in your heart of hearts
Sing with the energy, allow it to flow

Breathe it in to your inner depths
Feel it, Allow it, Dance with it

My Child
See your light
You are Divine as well

Janel

The lyrics *I Am Here* speaks of a self acceptance in ways I could never do before. It felt as though I was having a moment of awareness of where I came from. I knew what I could do for myself and for others. I felt safe here and I could blend all my feelings until they came together as one.

The last line reassures us how there is no limit in what we can access for ourselves and for others when our intention is pure.

I AM HERE

I am here to bring you light
I am here to bring you love
I am here to help you feel safe
I am here to help you heal

When you feel dark, breathe in light
When you feel hurt, breathe in healing
When you feel fear, breathe in love
When you feel pain, breathe in strength

Now that you know who I am
And I know who you are
We can be our highest intention
We can choose from afar

Many times lyrics would come to me while I was beginning to awaken. When that happened the feelings felt disjointed while I was in a dream state of mind. And then the visions would blend with the dreams.

The lyrics of *In My Dreams* are an example of such an event. I felt as though I had been dancing with the stars and God wrapped his arms around me to let me know that it was okay to feel safe and good in my personal space.

IN MY DREAMS

As I drift from place to place
There is a shining light
What is that light so bright?
What will it bring to me?

I have seen what has been
I have seen what is now
I have seen what could be
And still the light shines on

I have seen energy as love
As healing and truth
I have felt myself sitting
In a safe and soft golden space

There is that shining light again!
An Orb that is so bright
Who is that Divine Being?
Oh, I see it's me

I have talked about my beliefs and how I felt that it was important to experience the good as well as the bad. I have come to believe that it is not possible to know one without the other. That concept became clear to me when I started to think about diversity.

While I was growing up I had never known someone of another race or someone who had different ethnic beliefs. Of course I had read about them but I had never experienced any interaction. That led me to believe that I had never experienced diversity.

Then one day, I remembered what I had experienced and that was religious separation. I was raised in community school that was mainly Protestant, while another small town nearby was Catholic. When the kids in the Catholic school would get into trouble they would be sent to our school and our parents would say that we (their daughters) should stay away from those Catholic boys because they were always in trouble. I had an intense prejudice against Catholic boys.

Thanks to my interaction with 4-H and other community clubs, I found that my prejudice was unfounded. There were many very nice Catholic boys.

As strange as that may sound, you might imagine how shocked I was when people would tell me about their bad feelings towards someone of a different race. I had to sort through these new experiences on my own because I had nothing to compare them with from my childhood and adult experiences.

See how our beliefs are formed and changed? Our experiences form our beliefs. Our beliefs form our aspects. Experiences, beliefs and aspects are all a combination of good and bad.

Then I took it a step further and wondered why label anything good or bad, why not just call them experiences for learning. I was delighted to find that same thread of truth in some of the books I was drawn to.

My experiences had taught me about the good and the bad that some refer to as light energy and dark energy. I had been taught that they both are just energy and that they do not necessarily need to be harmful or separated.

I also believed light and dark energies would continue to be very important to our existence if we want to feel emotions. I asked myself how would I know happiness if I had never experienced sadness.

I also wondered if there might be a time when they should be brought back together, energetically within us.

I had the opportunity to read about light and dark energies being referred to as the OH and the AH. I wondered what it would be like to write a lyric about light and darkness as spiritual energies, then to allow them to join as though they were lost lovers. This lyric expresses those inspired thoughts and it is called *The OH & The AH.*

THE OH AND THE AH

(Joining Spiritual Darkness and Light)

OH greets AH with open arms
Like two branches spread
After the leaves are gone

As the last drop of fear fades away
The love of OH washes over AH
AH remembers the NOW

The AH has spent so much time
remembering only the battles,
staying far, far away; thinking
never to see OH again.

What a relief to know the secret
And feel what it's like to be
OH & AH together again
True lovers in the stars.

AH greets OH with open arms
Like two branches spread
With the leaves all aglow

Through my experiences I had discovered that finding enlightened contentment not only affected my emotions, my spirituality but my physical life as well.

Imagine for a moment that you are always in a state of contentment and you can sense every molecular cell within you. Take that moment and imagine you can talk with your cells, you can wake them up and let them live to their highest degree of fulfillment.

Why not express your heart felt intention for this right now? You could have your perfect life here on earth this moment. Then when you listen to heaven's music and celebrate finding your vision you just might gain understanding that everything you treasure is happening right Now!

The next lyrics *Intentions* were inspired by a simple awareness that everything was perfect just the way it was. That simple thought could bring a new normal to anyone who desires it.

INTENTION

My Intent is Pure
My Intent is Clear

I will not waver
I will not fear

There is much to acquire
There is much to admire

Where will you lead me
Where will I be

The heavens will open
You have spoken

I AM THAT I AM

Take me by the Hand
Let us be On Our Way

You may have heard of an alternative method called Body Talk of the healing arts. I have had good experiences with this method, it is very interesting. Feel free to check out the numerous web sites regarding this information.

This method played a big part in reminding me that I could communicate with my body. I liked the advice that I could tell my body to take care of itself, while my concentration was elsewhere. This concept worked very well for me because I believed and still believe that I am made up of a Body of Consciousness that includes my mind, body and spirit.

When there was an issue with my body I had a better recognition of what was going on. In other words I have learned to pay close attention to my body. My instincts tell me when to pay attention to what I am eating, or if I need more rest, or if I need more quiet time (not just for sleep). I have acquired an acute awareness and can also easily recognize when to seek professional help.

Interestingly enough, the lyrics to *Body Talk* repeated in my head for a few days before I wrote them down. I was enjoying the lightness of the music and the joy I felt when hearing the words in a tune that turned out to be similar to Cher singing *Turn Back Time*.

At this time I am not concerned about a disclaimer other than to say that my lyrics are very personal and if any of my lyrics would happen to end up in a song, the musical creation would most definitely be my own as well.

This lyrical entry called *Body Talk* felt very long to me even though there were very few words. Once it started playing in my mind it continued to play over and over.

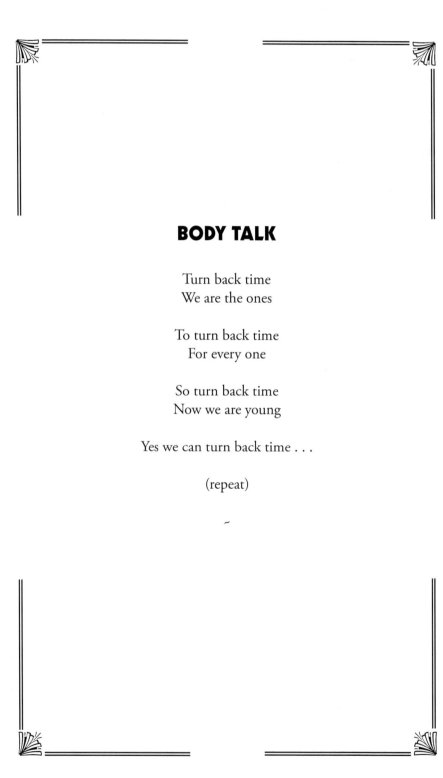

BODY TALK

Turn back time
We are the ones

To turn back time
For every one

So turn back time
Now we are young

Yes we can turn back time . . .

(repeat)

While communicating with my body and basically listening to my needs, I discovered that there was an overall experience I was having but I had not put it into words. Then it came to me.

First I would like to mention here that many of you may already be doing stretching and physical exercises consistent with your doctor's advice. That is how it should be. But when you have completed your physical exercises, there is another step that might interest you. That step is clearing, releasing and balancing your *body systems*.

My definition of body systems is based upon how I address my total body when I feel the need or desire to clear, release and balance myself. There are four systems that I have included in my routine and they are the Energetic System (Chakras); Skeletal System; Muscular System and Automated System (heart, lungs, brain, digestive and immune systems)

Before I begin the exercise; I take several deep breaths and clear all thoughts. I connect with my higher Source (God). Then I connect with the Earth (ground). Then I begin the process.

I visualize my body and focus on a system: Either the Energetic System (Chakras); Skeletal System; Muscular System or Automated System (heart, lungs, brain, digestive and immune systems).

I take a deep breath in—exhale through my mouth with sound or force whichever is most comfortable at the time, until I am breathing deeply but in a normal rhythm. As I go through the body systems and sense an imbalance, I return to the exhaling through the mouth. And then I return to a deep but normal breathing rhythm again.

When I have completed the process I can return to my daily functions feeling that I have cleared, released and balanced every Chakra, bone, muscle and organ in my physical and energetic body.

If you have serious health issues or have trouble breathing, check with your doctor before beginning any new exercise or program.

I had come to realize that breathing was not totally automatic for me at times such as when my exercise trainer was telling me to keep breathing. I call that conscious breathing and it can be very helpful when being distracted. I have learned not to confuse breathing less due to distractions with any type of sleep disorder. It is important to become aware of the differences.

Initially I started practicing deep breathing exercises because I found that it helped me relax, it helped me to feel less stressed. It quieted my mind. I found that if I was thinking about my breathing other thoughts could not bother me as much.

For instance when thoughts from a busy day were following me to bed at night and I couldn't get to sleep, deep breathing helped me to leave those thoughts behind and get a good night's sleep. I believed that as more time passed for me, the more important conscious breathing became.

An important point to make would be that I have come to realize there should be a balance to stress. As with everything else there is good stress and bad stress. I have found where my stress levels are and that was an important step in finding what works for me.

Now there are times when I feel as though breathing is not as necessary as it used to be. But then I remind myself that the reason is probably because I am still practicing deep breathing exercises. My exercises help me to be fully oxidized and my body could be reacting differently now.

I do not have any medical evidence to base this on, just my own perception.

What I do know for sure is that my experiences with my conscious breathing began to prompt a lyrical message to remind myself of the importance. The tune was very similar to Faith Hill's recording *Breathe Just Breathe*. Again these are my lyrics not hers.

BREATHE JUST BREATHE

When you're down and out
Can only cry and shout
Remember who you're not and
Breathe just breathe

When the day is long
You know you don't belong
Remember where you've been and
Breathe just breathe

When you turn around
And finally find the Sun
Remember you're the One and
Breathe just breathe

Remember, Remember, Remember
Breathe Just Breathe

I must admit that when I hear the music I have been mentioning it feels like heaven's music coming through to me. I am in awe of the beautiful souls who write music for other people's lyrics.

Then I remembered when I was studying music theory many years ago there was a class where I was required to write the parts for all the instruments in the orchestra. That was an exceptional assignment and I felt very proud when I looked at the completed musical manuscript. I do not believe that I am drawn to do anything like that composition again, but it is good to know that I can still recall the feelings associated with the memories.

During the next writing the music came in for me like a choir and just like before it was based on some other music I had heard and enjoyed. The music and lyrics of *Listen to the Choir* made me smile and enjoy the moments of just feeling.

During this time I had noticed that the common theme when reaching a point of feeling Enlightened Contentment is also the feeling that I AM One with the Universe.

LISTEN TO THE CHOIR

Listen to the choir, everyone
Listen to the choir, everyday
Listen to the choir, everyone
They sing We Are One

Do you want good health? It's alright
Do you want True Love?
With all your might
Do you want Abundance? It's alright
Now listen to your light

Listen to the Sound We Are One
Listen to the Sound everyday
Listen to the Sound We Are One
Yes listen, we are One

Sing in the choir everyone
Sing in the choir everyday
Sing in the choir everyone
Yes Sing We Are One

The concept of being one with everyone else brought me to the idea that I could live in the moment. I could see the beauty of the earth. I could hear the music of the birds, frogs and insects. I could feel the love and compassion others were sharing with me. I understood that I did not have to give my energy away without receiving the sweet energy in return. Those moments became so special and so precious that I felt a desire to remind myself to celebrate. I reminded myself that no matter where my journey had begun the important state of mind over matter for me was to be able to celebrate the fact that I could make choices. I could also make different choices when I felt I was not choosing what made my heart sing.

The lyrics to *Celebrate* reminded me to enjoy all the steps of the process and of the journey. I wanted to always remember to continue using the gift of choice. Making choices also meant to me that I would be feeling everything associated with each experience. (The good, the bad and the ugly)

CELEBRATE

Celebrate, celebrate,
Celebrate the NOW

When this journey began
We chose where we are

When this journey began
We knew our fears might come

Oh, we can choose again
Choose again to just be

How should we choose again?
Whatever we can be

Now I choose again
I choose Love, Light and Health

I choose Harmony, Peace and Wealth
So It Will Be

Celebrate, celebrate
Celebrate the Now

There were times after the celebrating calmed down that my chosen reality flooded into my mind. I realized that I had created my reality and that I could choose to change what no longer served me. That statement meant I could change my perception of what was happening in my world; in my mind.

One reality check I was reminded of was looking in the mirror and trying to find the younger version of who I was.

I know that everybody even the young, may look in the mirror and see someone they do not totally accept. Then they may apply make-up to enhance their beauty. They may change the color of their hair.

After making changes they may still be hearing negative voices in their head about their appearance. I know that has been my experience. (I could write a book about the issue of self acceptance, but that is for another time).

Ultimately we all forget that the beauty from within will shine through with or without makeup. Those are the times when I remind myself to let go of my old nagging self worth issues. And continue the process to release and let go of the notion that I am only what I see in the mirror.

Again I take a deep breath and change my perception of myself. Then when I look in the mirror I sense who I am and the person in the mirror looks softer, more loving and relaxed.

The message *You* reminded me how important it was to accept who I am, to accept others as well and to remind everyone to accept themselves, with or without make up.

YOU

See me as I appear to be and
Know it is okay to see you as
You appear to be.

See me as I Am and know
It is okay to see you as you are.
Then let go of who you see you are.

What is left?

Your I AM Presence

YOU as a Bright Star

Everything else is floating around
YOU
Within easy reach of your desires.

Choose what you wish for your Self
Always know it cannot touch you
Unless you choose to feel
Then let go and find
Your I AM Presence

YOU!

Accepting myself and others as they are leads me to relationships. Oh yes, the king and queen of issues for almost everyone I know. When I stopped to review, it occurred to me that most of my relationships were a give and take proposition.

The following thought enters most relationships, whether it is conscious or unconscious, "I will give you something if you will give me something in return." My relationships did not work well with this mind set. I went so far as to think I was put on this earth to devote my life to finding someone who needed me. I even thought it was my duty to help them become all they were meant to be. That included a mate and even some friends. In this type of relationship if the word *sharing* comes up, it becomes a sign that something is *wrong* in the relationship rather than a sign that something is *strong* in the relationship. For instance what reaction do you get when a mate or friend says "We need to talk." Most of you would say that you were thinking something was wrong.

Sharing and venting can become the way of life for some couples. The one doing the sharing and venting feels good after they let go of what is bothering them. The other feels down and depressed and wondering what hit them. With this mindset it is very difficult to find a common ground for sharing and venting. It would become difficult to face that bombardment every time you went home. Home would not feel like a safe place to be. Energetically it would feel as though they were taking turns being under attack.

What can be done to help each other vent when necessary? I have found that if I have prepared myself to be a sounding board, I accept the sharing and venting without it affecting me emotionally or physically. If I am not prepared energetically, I find myself giving unwanted advice. I have to recognize my feelings immediately and take the necessary steps to be a good listener.

A simple reminder is when you are feeling strong emotions about someone else's daily events you will need to stop, take a deep breath and wait for them to ask for your input. That advice is not easy for those of us who have strong maternal instincts, but it may help you to avoid a confrontation or melt down in your communications.

Here are some questions I have been asked about my personal feelings: "What are you creating in your relationships? Are you dependent on someone to make you happy? Do you want someone to complete you?" I had to take a good hard look at myself and ask "What is wrong with me that I think someone else can make me happy or complete me?"

I met a wise young lady at a seminar that asked me the question. "Where are you going and who do you want to take with you?" I immediately answered "My husband, even if he is kicking and screaming all the way." I laughed about that comment at the time, but later I realized that I would be forcing my husband to come with me on my journey rather than allowing him to find his own. I had to let go of that idea and change my perception of who I thought he was.

I knew that I had the opportunity to feel comfortable about myself and to be where I wanted to be. I was given the chance to know where I wanted to go and who I wanted to share my life with. It was clear I had to allow them to make the same choices. If someone wanted to join me on my journey, that would have to be their choice. The most important thing would be that they were making choices for themselves, to please themselves, not me. I knew that both of us would have to make ourselves happy and feel complete as a physical, emotional and spiritual being.

I was convinced that when life mates share all that they have energetically with each other, then they would have what they need in their relationship. That would be the moment they could say, "I have found someone who understands me and I understand them." That is when two people can share love by saying to each other, "Knowing who you are makes me happy." Isn't that what we are all striving for? Wouldn't that be the ideal relationship?

The poem *What's It Like* came to me when I became aware of my husband's effect on others especially children. When our granddaughters were in preschool he really enjoyed going to visit. I did too but I became more of a spectator as you will see.

As I watched their interaction I became filled with the magic of the moment. The granddaughters would race to hug him and urge him to sit with them and read a story. As he would begin reading the other children would flock to him and want to sit as close to him as they could. Love and light surrounded the whole scene and reached out and touched all who were watching. It was a marvelous, magical sight.

WHAT'S IT LIKE

What's it like to be you
So strong and so gentle
All at the same time

What's it like to feel the love
As the children run to hug you
And cling to you

What's it like to feel the pain
When you don't stop until you drop
And resting doesn't come easy

What's it like to feel the joy
As you talk with the children
As though you were one with them

What's it like to be you
So strong and so gentle
All at the same time

For the Love of my Life
Don,
From Jan

My husband and I have had many years together practicing our relationship. In fact at the time of this writing we have had thirty years of married life to reflect upon.

I believe that there is a light within all of us that shines out to those who are looking for answers, or seeking a comfortable and peaceful existence. This light when expanded guides many to find what they are searching for within themselves. I have seen this light in my husband and he has inspired me to write many poems in our time together.

Your Guiding Light was one of those poems written for him. It came to me one day when I was thinking about our 23rd wedding anniversary. I not only wanted to share with him my thoughts but I knew he was very impressed with the lighthouses we had seen on our vacation to New Hampshire. He had a fond memory of the beautiful serene villages along the coastline in Maine. As the inspiration began to flow, I took some photos from our trip and had them copied with the poem. He liked it.

YOUR GUIDING LIGHT

You are like a lighthouse
in so many special ways

Shining bright for all to see,
across the mighty waves

Those who are afraid or lost
will search for a guiding light

Some will look and see you
shining across the water blue

Many will be grateful;
very few will know it's you

Happy 23rd Anniversary

~

I have mentioned the word awareness several times throughout my writing. I realized how *awareness* was a significant factor in my personal growth. My journey consisted of many moments that can be called *aha* moments. These moments led to even deeper levels of awareness. A big aha moment came when I noticed the subtle differences between my being aware of my physical needs and being aware of my emotional feelings while releasing old experiences. It felt as though there was a flow to the energy. The poem *Awareness-Ebb and Flow* was the result of this inspiration.

AWARENESS—EBB AND FLOW

Awareness of the physical brings it nearer
Better perspective and understanding

Aha moments are like the physical,
Ebbing closer, becoming clearer.

Notice how awareness of your feelings
Allows them to drift afar

Where there is greater perspective and
Better understanding.

Memories are like your feelings,
Flowing afar

Spring Solstice 2012 will bring to completion 70 years since my birth. I like to say I will have completed 70 years because that is how we celebrate birthdays, isn't it?

I've always loved being a spring baby, the time for new growth and watching the buds begin and continue to grow into beautiful blooms. Spring has always brought inspiration to my heart and soul. I look forward to writing about it each year.

The winter of 2011 was very long and cold with very deep snow in the Mid Western states. I hope you can feel the beauty of the seasons as well as the warmth in my soul with *Here Comes the Spring* 2011

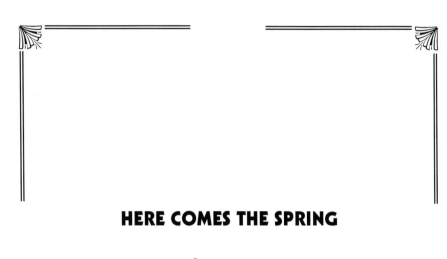

HERE COMES THE SPRING

Iowa winters
Long and harsh
The snow, the ice and
The wind that howls

The sculptures created by
This magnificent power
Is a magical scene of our
Winter Wonderland

Iowa springs wet and strong
With fears of floods; a
Forever changed landscape
That lingers on and on

Beauty is created by the massive rain
Brings green fields and leaves
Flowers pushing up to meet the sun
Birds return to sing and chatter
A reminder that we are All One

I ask the Lord to shower me
With gifts; being careful not to whine
About a seemingly tiny wish

I hear His gentle voice

Your wish is my command;
I empower thee with
Love, Compassion, and
Endless Potentials
Of these, the greatest gift is
Love

THESE THINGS I KNOW:

This is the time to pull all this information together into one elongated thought: If you choose to know more about your connection to your Soul, you will find that you are beginning a New Age, that you can set a new standard and a new normal for yourself. You will discover enlightened contentment; you will be a Body of Consciousness (mind, body and soul). You will live your New Passion while experiencing, expanding and expressing.

Living your Passion is Energy in Motion.

Because I chose to seek knowledge and wisdom, I found that in this New Age of discovering Enlightened Contentment I have become a New Consciousness Master teaching a New Standard of living through my New Passion for words. I do this with love in my heart and with the intention that it is for the good of all humanity.

- ❖ Divine Intelligence is Imagination.
- ❖ Live life as though there are many tomorrows.
- ❖ Live each day one at a time completely
- ❖ Engage your Mind, Heart and Body Connection
- ❖ Live, Laugh, Love!
- ❖ Experience, Expand, Express!
- ❖ Express your joy, your hope and your **love** all around.

LOVE

Always remember
Love is a state of being
Not a means to an end
Love is a light flowing energy
Not a quick moment of force
Love will always shine from me to you
With a never ending source

Love is experiencing
Love is expanding
Love is expressing
JOY

My greatest hope is that you will find that you are empowered to be on
your way to your NEW Beginnings with your *energy in motion!*

(The End or)
New Beginnings

©Jan Hein 2011

DISCLAIMER

I am not responsible or liable for other's interpretation of these writings. This writing is based solely on my personal experiences that I am willing to share. I do not and will not give advice to others regarding their physical and mental health, or how to live their lives. My intentions are to present other perspectives and to inspire and invite others to find their own truth.

Janet R. Hein

CREDENTIALS

BA in Secondary Education
The Reconnection™ Level III Facilitator
Sedona Method® Graduate-Alternative Therapy
Eleuthera Synchrotize System™ Alternative Therapy
Certified Channel—Intuitive Guidance
New Consciousness Master—Educator
Published Author: Prose and short story

BIOGRAPHY OF
PUBLISHED WORKS

2004—Published in International Library of Poetry <u>The Silent Journey.</u> Editor's Choice award for poem "Dance with the Energy"

2005—Published in International Society of Poets <u>The Best Poems and Poets of 2004</u>. "When You Left"

2005—Published in Noble House Publishers <u>Labours of Love</u> "Memories of the Ocean"

2005—January –Published in International Society of Poets <u>Twilight Musings</u>. Editor's Choice award for poem "Take a Moment"

2006, December—2007, January issue of *Pet Folio* magazine-Article Published "Catch That Cat *on film*"